Cutting the Cord: A Practical Guide to Alternatives to Expensive Cable Television

Copyright Page

TITLE: Cutting the Cord: A Practical Guide to Alternatives to Expensive Cable Television

1ST Edition

Copyright @ 2023

ISBN: 9798223315599

Table of Contents

Cutting the Cord: A Practical Guide to Alternatives to Expensive Cable Television

By Roberto Miguel Rodriguez

Chapter 1: Understanding Cable Television and the Need for Alternatives

The High Costs and Limitations of Cable TV

Cable TV has long been a staple in households across the country, offering a wide range of channels and on-demand content. However, as technology advances and alternatives to expensive cable television become more readily available, it's becoming increasingly clear that the costs and limitations of cable TV are not worth the investment.

One of the biggest drawbacks of cable TV is the exorbitant costs associated with it. Cable subscription fees continue to rise year after year, leaving many households struggling to keep up with the expense. In addition to the basic package, there are often additional fees for premium channels, DVR service, and equipment rentals. When you add it all up, the total cost of cable TV can be astronomical.

Furthermore, cable TV often comes with long-term contracts and hidden fees. Many providers lock customers into contracts for a set period of time, making it difficult to cancel or switch to a more affordable alternative. Additionally, there are often fees for installation, equipment upgrades, and even cancellation. These hidden costs can quickly add up and leave consumers feeling trapped and financially burdened.

Another limitation of cable TV is the lack of flexibility and customization. With cable, you are limited to the channels and content provided by your provider. This means that you may be paying for channels that you never watch, while missing out on others that you would enjoy. Cable TV also lacks the convenience of on-demand streaming, which allows viewers to watch their favorite shows and movies whenever and wherever they want.

Fortunately, there are numerous alternatives to expensive cable television that offer more flexibility and affordability. Streaming services like Netflix, Hulu, and Amazon Prime provide a vast library of TV shows and movies for a fraction of the cost of cable TV. These platforms can be accessed through smart TVs, streaming devices like Roku or Amazon Fire Stick, or even on mobile devices.

Another option is using an antenna to receive free over-the-air channels. With a simple antenna setup, you can access local channels and enjoy high-definition programming without any monthly fees. This is a great option for those who only watch a few channels regularly and want to eliminate the recurring costs of cable TV.

IPTV services are another alternative worth exploring. These services utilize internet protocol to deliver a wide range of channels at a fraction of the cost of cable TV. With step-by-step instructions, you can set up and use IPTV services to access a variety of channels and content tailored to your preferences.

For those looking for free options, there are legal websites that provide access to a variety of TV shows and movies without any subscription fees. These sites offer a range of content, from classic shows to recent releases, and can be a great way to save money while still enjoying your favorite programs.

Other alternatives include creating a personal media server using a computer or a network-attached storage (NAS) device, exploring local library resources that offer DVDs, audiobooks, and online streaming platforms for free, or joining or creating local community networks or platforms where people share media content with one another.

In conclusion, cable TV may have been the go-to option for years, but the high costs and limitations associated with it are no longer worth the investment. With a wide range of alternatives available, from streaming services to antenna setups and DIY media servers, consumers can now find more affordable and flexible options to suit their needs. By cutting the cord and exploring these alternatives, you can take control of your entertainment options and save money in the process.

The Rise of Cord-Cutting and the Need for Alternatives

In recent years, there has been a significant shift in how people consume television content. The traditional cable television model, once the dominant force in the industry, is losing its appeal as consumers seek more affordable and flexible options. This trend, known as cord-cutting, has led to a growing need for alternatives to expensive cable television.

For those looking to cut the cord and explore alternatives, there are numerous options available. This subchapter will provide a comprehensive guide to help you navigate the world of cord-cutting and find the best alternative that suits your needs.

One popular alternative is streaming services. Platforms like Netflix, Hulu, and Amazon Prime offer a vast library of TV shows and movies at a fraction of the cost of cable TV. We will walk you through the process of setting up and using these popular streaming services, ensuring you can enjoy your favorite content without breaking the bank.

Another alternative is antenna TV setup. By installing an antenna, you can receive free over-the-air channels, including major networks like ABC, CBS, NBC, and more. Our step-by-step instructions will guide you through the antenna installation process, allowing you to access a wide range of channels without any subscription fees.

Smart TVs also offer built-in apps and features that can provide access to free or low-cost content. We will provide a comprehensive guide on how to utilize these apps and features, ensuring you can make the most of your smart TV and enjoy a variety of entertainment options without the need for cable TV.

IPTV services are another cost-effective alternative. These services offer a wide range of channels at a fraction of the cost of cable TV. Our step-by-step instructions will help you set up and use these internet protocol television services, allowing you to access a vast selection of channels and save money in the process.

In addition to these alternatives, we will explore free online streaming websites, DIY media server setups, Roku or Fire Stick setups, mobile streaming options, local library resources, and community-driven media sharing. Each of these alternatives offers unique benefits and can help you break free from the costly grip of cable television.

By exploring these alternatives, you can take control of your television viewing experience and save money in the process. Whether you choose to stream content, set up an antenna, utilize smart TV apps, or explore other alternatives, this subchapter will equip you with the knowledge and tools to embrace cord-cutting and find the best alternative to expensive cable television.

Benefits of Cutting the Cord: Saving Money and Gaining Flexibility

In today's digital age, the traditional cable television model is becoming increasingly expensive and rigid. As a result, more and more people are considering cutting the cord and exploring alternative options for their television viewing needs. This subchapter explores the various benefits that come with cutting the cord, including saving money and gaining flexibility.

One of the most significant advantages of cutting the cord is the potential for substantial cost savings. Cable television subscriptions can be exorbitantly expensive, with monthly bills quickly adding up. By switching to alternative options, individuals can significantly reduce their entertainment expenses. Whether it's utilizing streaming services like Netflix, Hulu, or Amazon Prime, setting up an antenna to receive free over-the-air channels, or exploring free online streaming websites, cord-cutters have access to a wide range of affordable or even free content.

Moreover, cutting the cord provides viewers with unprecedented flexibility. Traditional cable TV packages often come with a multitude of channels that go unused, leaving viewers paying for content they don't want or need. With streaming services, individuals can choose from a vast catalog of shows and movies and only pay for the services they actually use. This flexibility extends to the devices used for streaming as well. Smart TVs, Roku, Amazon Fire Stick, and mobile devices all provide convenient platforms for accessing streaming services, allowing viewers to watch their favorite shows and movies whenever and wherever they want.

Additionally, cutting the cord opens up opportunities for community-driven media sharing. Joining or creating local community networks or platforms where people share media content, such as TV shows or movies, with one another for free or at a low cost, allows individuals to connect with like-minded individuals and discover new content that might not be available through traditional cable TV.

In conclusion, cutting the cord offers numerous benefits to individuals looking for alternatives to expensive cable television. By saving money and gaining flexibility, viewers can tailor their entertainment experiences to their preferences and budgets. Whether it's through streaming services, antenna TV setups, smart TV apps and features, IPTV services, free online streaming websites, DIY media server setups, or community-driven media sharing, cutting the cord opens up a world of possibilities for cost-effective and personalized television viewing.

Factors to Consider Before Cutting the Cord: Internet Connection, Content Preferences, and Device Compatibility

In today's increasingly digital age, many individuals are looking for alternatives to expensive cable television. Cutting the cord has become a popular choice for those seeking more affordable and flexible options for accessing their favorite TV shows and movies. However, before you make the leap, there are several factors to consider to ensure a smooth transition and maximize your cord-cutting experience.

First and foremost, it is essential to evaluate your internet connection. Streaming services rely heavily on a stable and fast internet connection to deliver high-quality content. Before cutting the cord, check your current internet plan to ensure it offers sufficient bandwidth for streaming. If necessary, consider upgrading to a higher speed plan to avoid buffering or lagging issues.

Another crucial factor to consider is your content preferences. Take some time to reflect on the shows, movies, and channels that are must-haves for you and your family. Research the availability of these options on different streaming platforms and alternative services to ensure you can access your favorite content without cable. Services like Netflix, Hulu, Amazon Prime, or IPTV providers offer a wide range of channels and on-demand content, but it's important to verify if they offer the specific programming you desire.

Device compatibility is also a significant consideration. Assess the devices you currently own, such as smart TVs, streaming devices like Roku or Amazon Fire Stick, smartphones, or tablets. Ensure that these devices are compatible with the streaming platforms or services you plan to use. If necessary, invest in additional devices or upgrades to optimize your streaming experience.

Furthermore, it's worth exploring free or low-cost alternatives to cable TV, such as antenna TV, free online streaming websites, and local library resources. Antenna TV setup can grant you access to free over-the-air channels, while legal streaming websites offer a variety of TV shows and movies without any subscription fees. Local libraries often provide DVDs, audiobooks, and online streaming platforms for free, expanding your content options even further.

By considering these factors, you can make an informed decision before cutting the cord and embark on your journey to alternative, cost-effective television options. Whether you choose to rely on streaming services, antenna TV, DIY media servers, or community-driven media sharing platforms, understanding your internet connection, content preferences, and device compatibility will ensure a seamless transition and an enjoyable cord-cutting experience.

Chapter 2: Exploring Streaming Services as Cable TV Alternatives

Introduction to Streaming Services: Netflix, Hulu, and Amazon Prime

In this subchapter, we will delve into the exciting world of streaming services, specifically focusing on three popular platforms: Netflix, Hulu, and Amazon Prime. Streaming services have revolutionized the way we consume entertainment, offering a wide range of TV shows, movies, and documentaries at the click of a button. With their extensive libraries and user-friendly interfaces, these platforms have become go-to alternatives for expensive cable television.

Netflix, Hulu, and Amazon Prime have become household names, providing a vast array of content to suit every taste and preference. Netflix, for instance, boasts an extensive catalog of TV shows and movies, including original productions that have garnered critical acclaim. Hulu, on the other hand, offers a combination of current shows, classic series, and original content, making it an excellent choice for those who want to keep up with the latest episodes. Lastly, Amazon Prime Video provides not only a wide range of movies and TV shows but also exclusive access to original productions and a vast library of content available for rent or purchase.

One of the key advantages of streaming services is the flexibility they offer. Unlike cable television, which requires a fixed schedule, streaming services allow you to watch your favorite shows and movies on-demand, at any time and from any device with an internet connection. This convenience has made streaming services particularly appealing to cord-cutters, individuals who have decided to abandon traditional cable TV in favor of more cost-effective alternatives.

Throughout this subchapter, we will explore the features and functionalities of these streaming platforms, providing step-by-step instructions on how to sign up, navigate their interfaces, and make the most of their vast content libraries. We will also discuss the various subscription options available, including family plans and premium add-ons, allowing you to customize your streaming experience to fit your needs and preferences.

Whether you are new to streaming services or looking to expand your knowledge, this subchapter will serve as a comprehensive guide to using Netflix, Hulu, and Amazon Prime as alternatives to expensive cable television. By the end of this chapter, you will have a solid understanding of how to maximize your streaming experience, saving both time and money while enjoying a wide range of high-quality content. So, let's dive in and explore the world of streaming services!

Choosing the Right Streaming Service for Your Needs

In today's digital age, the options for watching television and movies have expanded far beyond traditional cable television. With the rise of streaming services and other alternatives, cutting the cord has become a popular choice for many households looking to save money without sacrificing their favorite shows and movies. However, with so many options available, it can be overwhelming to choose the right streaming service for your needs. In this chapter, we will explore the various factors to consider when selecting a streaming service and provide recommendations based on different preferences and interests.

First and foremost, it's essential to determine what type of content you enjoy watching. Are you a movie buff, a sports enthusiast, or a binge-watcher of TV series? Different streaming services cater to these preferences, with some specializing in movies, while others focus on TV shows or sports events. For movie lovers, popular options like Netflix, Hulu, and Amazon Prime Video offer extensive libraries of films in various genres. Sports fans may prefer services like ESPN+ or fuboTV, which provide live streaming of sporting events and exclusive sports content. If you're a TV series aficionado, platforms like HBO Max, Disney+, or Apple TV+ offer a wide range of original shows and popular series.

Another crucial factor to consider is the cost and flexibility of the streaming service. While most services require a monthly subscription fee, the prices can vary significantly. It's important to evaluate your budget and determine how much you are willing to spend on entertainment. Additionally, consider whether you prefer contracts or commitments. Some services offer monthly subscriptions that can be canceled anytime, while others require annual commitments. If you're unsure, many services provide free trial periods, allowing you to test their offerings before committing long-term.

Furthermore, take into account the devices you plan to use for streaming. Most streaming services are accessible on multiple platforms, including smart TVs, computers, smartphones, and tablets. However, it's always a good idea to ensure that the service you choose is compatible with your preferred devices to avoid any compatibility issues.

Lastly, consider the additional features and benefits that streaming services offer. Some services provide offline viewing, allowing you to download content and watch it without an internet connection. Others offer personalized recommendations based on your viewing history, making it easier to discover new shows and movies that match your interests.

By taking these factors into account, you can choose the right streaming service that aligns with your entertainment needs, budget, and preferences. Whether you're looking for a wide selection of movies, exclusive TV shows, live sports events, or a combination of all three, there is a streaming service out there that will cater to your needs. So, why continue paying for expensive cable television when you can enjoy a vast array of content at a fraction of the cost? Start exploring the world of streaming services today and embrace the freedom of cutting the cord.

Navigating Streaming Platforms: Interface and Features

In the digital age, there are countless alternatives to expensive cable television. One of the most popular options is streaming platforms, which offer a wide range of content at a fraction of the cost. However, for those new to streaming, understanding the interface and features of these platforms can be a bit overwhelming. This subchapter will provide a comprehensive guide on how to navigate streaming platforms like Netflix, Hulu, or Amazon Prime.

First, let's start with the basics of streaming platform interfaces. Upon logging in, you will be greeted with a user-friendly home screen that showcases featured content, personalized recommendations, and trending shows or movies. You can easily browse through different genres, search for specific titles, or explore curated collections.

Many streaming platforms also offer advanced features to enhance your viewing experience. One such feature is the ability to create multiple user profiles. This allows each member of your household to have their own personalized recommendations and watch history. Additionally, you can set parental controls to restrict certain content from being accessed by younger viewers.

Another important aspect to consider is the availability of subtitles and audio descriptions. Most streaming platforms provide a variety of language options and accessibility features to cater to diverse audiences. You can easily enable or customize these settings to suit your preferences.

Furthermore, streaming platforms often offer additional features to enhance your viewing experience. For example, Netflix allows you to download select shows and movies for offline viewing, perfect for long flights or areas with limited internet access. Amazon Prime Video offers X-Ray, a feature that provides IMDb information about the actors, music, and trivia while you watch.

It's also worth mentioning that streaming platforms regularly update their content libraries. New releases and exclusive shows are added frequently, ensuring that you never run out of options. Some platforms even produce their own original content, which has gained critical acclaim in recent years.

In conclusion, streaming platforms offer a diverse range of content with user-friendly interfaces and exciting features. By understanding how to navigate these platforms, you can access a plethora of streaming services and enjoy your favorite shows and movies at a fraction of the cost of cable TV. So, sit back, relax, and start exploring the world of streaming!

Setting Up and Managing Streaming Accounts

In this subchapter, we will delve into the world of streaming accounts and provide step-by-step instructions on how to set them up and manage them effectively. Streaming accounts are an essential part of cord-cutting, as they provide access to a wide range of content without the need for expensive cable subscriptions. Whether you're a beginner or a seasoned cord-cutter, this guide will provide you with the knowledge and tools to navigate popular streaming platforms and make the most out of your streaming experience.

We will start by introducing you to the concept of streaming services and the benefits they offer over traditional cable television. We will discuss popular platforms such as Netflix, Hulu, and Amazon Prime, explaining how to sign up, create profiles, and explore their vast libraries of TV shows, movies, and original content. We will also provide tips on optimizing your streaming experience, such as adjusting video quality settings and managing multiple accounts for different family members.

Next, we will explore antenna TV setup, which allows you to receive free over-the-air channels. We will provide detailed instructions on how to install and use an antenna, ensuring you have access to local news, sports, and other broadcast channels without paying a dime.

For those with smart TVs, we will provide a comprehensive guide on utilizing the built-in apps and features to access free or low-cost content. From streaming platforms to free channels and apps, we will cover everything you need to know to make the most out of your smart TV's capabilities.

Internet Protocol Television (IPTV) services are gaining popularity among cord-cutters due to their extensive channel offerings at a fraction of the cost of cable TV. We will walk you through the process of setting up and using IPTV services, ensuring you have access to a wide range of channels from around the world.

Additionally, we will explore free online streaming websites that provide legal access to a variety of TV shows and movies without any subscription fees. We will recommend reliable and reputable websites, ensuring you can enjoy your favorite content without any legal or security risks.

Furthermore, we will guide you through the process of setting up a DIY media server using a computer or a network-attached storage (NAS) device. This will allow you to stream content to multiple devices within your home network, creating a personalized and convenient media experience.

Lastly, we will provide step-by-step instructions on setting up and optimizing popular streaming devices like Roku or Amazon Fire Stick.

These devices offer access to a plethora of streaming services, and we will ensure you have a seamless and enjoyable streaming experience.

By the end of this subchapter, you will have all the knowledge and tools necessary to set up and manage your streaming accounts effectively. Whether you prefer streaming on your smart TV, mobile devices, or through dedicated streaming devices, this guide will empower you to make the most out of the alternatives to expensive cable television.

Maximizing Streaming Quality and Performance

In the digital age, streaming has become the go-to method for consuming television shows and movies. As more people look for alternatives to expensive cable television, it's crucial to maximize streaming quality and performance to ensure an enjoyable viewing experience. Whether you're using popular streaming platforms like Netflix, Hulu, or Amazon Prime, setting up an antenna for free over-the-air channels, or exploring IPTV services, here are some tips to enhance your streaming experience.

First and foremost, ensure a stable internet connection. Streaming requires a reliable and fast internet connection to avoid buffering and lagging. Consider upgrading your internet plan or investing in a high-speed internet service to ensure smooth playback.

Optimize your home network. If you're experiencing issues with streaming quality, it might be due to a congested network. Make sure your router is placed in an optimal location and consider using a wired connection for better stability. Additionally, limit the number of devices connected to your network while streaming to allocate more bandwidth to your streaming device.

Regularly update your streaming apps and devices. Streaming platforms and devices often release updates to improve performance and fix bugs.

Stay up to date with the latest versions to ensure optimal streaming quality.

Adjust streaming settings. Most streaming platforms allow you to adjust the video quality based on your internet speed. If you're experiencing buffering issues, consider lowering the video quality or choosing a lower resolution option. Additionally, some platforms allow you to download content for offline viewing, which can save bandwidth and ensure a smooth playback experience.

Invest in a streaming device. While smart TVs often come with built-in streaming apps, using a dedicated streaming device like Roku or Amazon Fire Stick can provide a better streaming experience. These devices are designed to handle streaming content efficiently and often offer additional features and apps.

Consider using a virtual private network (VPN). A VPN can improve your streaming experience by eliminating any throttling or buffering issues caused by your internet service provider. It can also enhance your security and protect your privacy while streaming.

Lastly, make sure your streaming device is properly configured. Check for any available firmware updates, optimize your device's settings, and clear cache regularly to keep your device running smoothly.

By following these tips, you can maximize your streaming quality and performance, ensuring a seamless and enjoyable viewing experience. Whether you're using popular streaming platforms, setting up an antenna, exploring IPTV services, or utilizing other alternatives, you can cut the cord on expensive cable television without sacrificing the quality of your entertainment.

Chapter 3: Harnessing the Power of Antenna TV

Understanding Over-the-Air Channels: What You Can Receive for Free

In today's world, cable television has become increasingly expensive, leaving many people searching for alternative options. One of the best alternatives to expensive cable television is over-the-air channels, which can be received for free. In this subchapter, we will explore the wonders of over-the-air channels and what they can offer you.

Over-the-air channels are broadcasted through the airwaves and can be received by using an antenna. The great news is that these channels are completely free, meaning you can enjoy a wide variety of content without having to pay hefty subscription fees. But what channels can you receive for free?

The answer is quite surprising. With an over-the-air antenna, you can access major broadcast networks such as ABC, CBS, NBC, FOX, and PBS. These networks offer a range of popular shows, news programs, sports events, and even live performances. You won't miss out on your favorite shows or the latest news updates.

Moreover, over-the-air channels also provide access to subchannels, which are additional channels within the main broadcast channels. These subchannels often offer specialized content, including classic TV shows, movies, music, and even educational programs. It's like having a whole new world of entertainment right at your fingertips.

Setting up an antenna for over-the-air channels is easier than you might think. In this subchapter, we will provide you with step-by-step instructions on how to install and use an antenna effectively. From finding the best location for your antenna to optimizing the signal reception, we will guide you through the process.

Over-the-air channels are just one of the many alternatives to expensive cable television. In this book, we also cover other options such as streaming services, smart TV apps, IPTV services, free online streaming websites, DIY media servers, streaming devices like Roku or Amazon Fire Stick, mobile streaming options, local library resources, and community-driven media sharing platforms.

By exploring these alternatives, you can save a significant amount of money while still enjoying your favorite TV shows, movies, and sports events. It's time to take control of your entertainment options and cut the cord with expensive cable television. Stay tuned for more valuable information on how to make the most of these alternatives in the following chapters.

Choosing the Right Antenna: Types and Considerations

In this subchapter, we will explore the different types of antennas available and provide considerations for selecting the right one to access free over-the-air channels. With the rising popularity of alternatives to expensive cable television, using an antenna has become a cost-effective solution for accessing local channels and saving money on monthly bills. This information is tailored to the public, specifically those interested in cord-cutting and exploring alternative options for their entertainment needs.

Types of Antennas:

1. Indoor Antennas: These compact antennas are designed to be placed inside your home, typically near a window or in an area with good reception. They are easy to install and ideal for urban areas with strong signal strength.

2. Outdoor Antennas: These larger antennas are installed on the roof or outside a building. They offer better reception and are suitable for areas with weaker signals or rural locations.

Considerations for Choosing an Antenna:

1. Signal Strength: Before selecting an antenna, it is important to determine the signal strength in your area. Websites like AntennaWeb or TV Fool provide information on signal availability and strength based on your location.

2. Range: Antennas have different ranges, which determine the distance they can receive signals from. Consider the proximity of broadcasting towers and select an antenna with an appropriate range for your location.

3. Multi-Directional vs. Directional: Multi-directional antennas receive signals from various directions, making them suitable for areas with broadcasting towers in different locations. Directional antennas focus on signals from a specific direction and are ideal if all the towers are in one direction.

4. Amplification: Antennas with built-in amplifiers enhance weak signals, improving reception. If you live far from broadcasting towers or encounter obstacles like buildings or trees, an amplified antenna may be necessary.

5. Installation and Setup: Consider the ease of installation and the antenna's compatibility with your TV or streaming device. Some antennas require professional installation, while others can be easily set up by following step-by-step instructions.

By understanding the different types of antennas and considering factors such as signal strength, range, and installation requirements, you can choose the right antenna to access free over-the-air channels. This is an essential step in your journey to cutting the cord and exploring alternative options for your television needs.

Installing and Positioning Your Antenna for Optimal Reception

When it comes to cutting the cord and finding alternatives to expensive cable television, one of the best options is installing an antenna to receive free over-the-air channels. Not only does this give you access to local news, sports, and popular network shows, but it also provides a crystal-clear high-definition picture without the need for a monthly subscription.

To get started, you'll need an antenna that is suitable for your location and the channels you want to receive. There are two types of antennas to choose from: indoor and outdoor. Indoor antennas are more convenient and easier to install, while outdoor antennas generally provide better reception and access to more channels. Consider factors such as distance from broadcast towers, terrain, and obstructions when selecting the right antenna for your needs.

Once you have your antenna, the next step is positioning it for optimal reception. Start by finding the best location in your home, preferably near a window or wall facing the direction of the nearest broadcast towers. Higher placement, such as on the roof or in the attic, can also improve reception. Avoid placing the antenna near electronic devices or metal objects that can interfere with the signal.

After finding the ideal location, connect the antenna to your television using a coaxial cable. Make sure the cable is securely attached to both the antenna and the TV. Then, go to your TV's menu and select the option to scan for channels. This will allow your TV to search for available channels and save them for easy access.

If you're not getting the desired reception, try adjusting the position and direction of the antenna. Small movements can make a significant difference in signal strength. You can also try rotating the antenna to find the best angle for receiving signals. Additionally, consider using an amplifier or signal booster if you're located far from broadcast towers or if there are obstructions in your area.

Remember, the number and quality of channels you receive can vary depending on your location. It's a good idea to visit websites like AntennaWeb.org or TV Fool to determine the available channels in your area and the type of antenna you need.

By following these step-by-step instructions and taking into account the specific factors affecting your location, you can install and position your antenna for optimal reception. Enjoy the benefits of free over-the-air channels and join the growing community of cord-cutters who have found alternatives to expensive cable television.

Scanning for Channels and Managing Your Over-the-Air TV Setup

In this subchapter, we will dive into the world of over-the-air TV and explore the various ways you can scan for channels and optimize your setup. Over-the-air TV allows you to access free, high-quality broadcast channels without the need for an expensive cable subscription. This is a great option for those looking to cut the cord and save money on their monthly bills.

To begin, let's discuss the basics of antenna TV setup. We will provide you with step-by-step instructions on how to install and use an antenna to receive free over-the-air channels. From choosing the right antenna for your location to finding the best spot for optimal signal reception, we will guide you through the entire process. We will also explain how to scan for channels and organize them for easy navigation.

Next, we will explore the smart TV apps and features that can enhance your over-the-air TV experience. Many modern smart TVs come with built-in apps and features that provide access to free or low-cost content. We will provide you with a comprehensive guide on how to utilize these apps and features to maximize your viewing options.

If you're looking for even more channel options, we will explain how to set up and use internet protocol television (IPTV) services. IPTV services offer a wide range of channels at a fraction of the cost of cable TV. We will provide you with step-by-step instructions on how to set up and navigate these services to expand your viewing choices.

Additionally, we will explore free online streaming websites that offer access to a variety of TV shows and movies without any subscription fees. We will provide you with a list of legal websites that you can explore for a wide range of content options.

For those who prefer a more DIY approach, we will delve into the world of creating a personal media server. We will guide you through the process of setting up a media server using a computer or a network-attached storage (NAS) device. With a personal media server, you can stream content to multiple devices within your home network.

Finally, we will discuss popular streaming devices like Roku or Amazon Fire Stick. We will provide step-by-step instructions on how to set up and optimize these devices to access a plethora of streaming services. These devices can greatly enhance your streaming experience and provide access to a wide range of content options.

Whether you're new to cord-cutting or looking to expand your options, this subchapter will provide you with the knowledge and tools to scan for channels and manage your over-the-air TV setup effectively. By exploring these alternatives to expensive cable television, you can save money while still enjoying a wide variety of entertainment options.

Chapter 4: Making the Most of Smart TV Apps and Features

Exploring the Built-in Apps and Features of Smart TVs

In today's digital age, smart TVs have revolutionized the way we consume entertainment. These advanced televisions come equipped with a range of built-in apps and features that can provide access to a wealth of free or low-cost content. In this subchapter, we will delve into the world of smart TV apps and features, empowering you to make the most of your device and cut the cord on expensive cable television.

Smart TVs are essentially televisions with integrated internet connectivity, allowing you to access a wide range of online content. From streaming services like Netflix, Hulu, or Amazon Prime to free online streaming websites, the possibilities are endless. We will guide you through the process of navigating these apps, signing up for subscriptions, and exploring the vast libraries of TV shows and movies available at your fingertips.

Additionally, we will discuss the benefits of setting up an antenna TV system to receive free over-the-air channels. By combining the use of your smart TV with an antenna, you can access local channels and enjoy live broadcasts without any subscription fees. We will provide step-by-step instructions on installing and using an antenna, ensuring that you have a seamless viewing experience.

Furthermore, we will introduce you to the concept of IPTV services. By utilizing internet protocol television, you can access a wide range of channels at a fraction of the cost of cable TV. We will provide detailed instructions on setting up and using IPTV services, allowing you to explore an extensive selection of content without breaking the bank.

For tech-savvy individuals, we will offer a comprehensive guide on creating a personal media server using a computer or a network-attached storage (NAS) device. This DIY media server setup will enable you to stream content to multiple devices within your home, offering a convenient and cost-effective alternative to cable TV.

Lastly, we will explore the various media resources available at local libraries, including DVDs, audiobooks, and online streaming platforms. Many libraries offer these resources for free, allowing you to access a wide range of content without any subscription fees.

By delving into the built-in apps and features of smart TVs, you can unlock a world of free or low-cost entertainment options. Whether you're interested in streaming services, antenna TV, IPTV, DIY media servers, or local library resources, this subchapter will provide you with the step-by-step instructions and guidance you need to cut the cord on expensive cable television and embrace a more affordable and flexible approach to entertainment.

Configuring and Customizing Smart TV Settings

In today's digital age, Smart TVs have become an integral part of our entertainment system. These cutting-edge devices offer a wide range of features and applications that can enhance our viewing experience. In this subchapter, we will explore how to configure and customize Smart TV settings to make the most of these advanced functionalities.

To begin with, let's delve into the initial setup process. When you first turn on your Smart TV, it will guide you through a series of prompts to connect to your home network. Make sure to have your Wi-Fi credentials handy to establish a stable internet connection.

Once connected, it's time to personalize your Smart TV experience. Start by adjusting the display settings to suit your preferences. You can modify aspects such as brightness, contrast, and color saturation to achieve the optimal picture quality.

Next, let's explore the audio settings. Here, you can fine-tune the sound output to your liking. Adjust the volume levels, enable surround sound, or experiment with different audio modes to create an immersive audio experience.

Moving on, let's delve into the Smart TV interface. Most Smart TVs allow you to customize the home screen, making it easier to access your favorite apps and channels. Rearrange the icons, remove unnecessary ones, and prioritize the applications you use the most.

Furthermore, Smart TVs often come with built-in apps and streaming services. Take the time to explore these offerings and discover a world of free or low-cost content. Popular platforms like Netflix, Hulu, and Amazon Prime provide an abundance of TV shows and movies at your fingertips.

Moreover, Smart TVs can also be integrated with other devices in your home network. By connecting your smartphone, tablet, or computer, you can effortlessly stream media to your TV screen. Create a personal media server using a computer or network-attached storage (NAS) device to access your digital library from anywhere in your home.

Lastly, don't forget to regularly update your Smart TV's firmware to ensure optimal performance and security. Manufacturers often release software updates that introduce new features and fix bugs, so it's vital to stay up to date.

By configuring and customizing your Smart TV settings, you can unlock its full potential and enjoy a personalized and immersive entertainment experience. Whether it's streaming your favorite shows, accessing free online content, or setting up a media server, your Smart TV has the power to revolutionize your cord-cutting journey. So, dive in and explore the endless possibilities that await you.

Accessing Free and Low-Cost Content through Smart TV Apps

In today's digital age, cutting the cord from expensive cable television has become a popular trend among the public. With the advancements in technology and the rise of streaming services, there are now numerous alternatives available that provide access to a wide range of entertainment at a fraction of the cost. One such alternative is utilizing the built-in apps and features of smart TVs to access free or low-cost content.

Smart TVs have revolutionized the way we consume media. These televisions come equipped with a variety of pre-installed apps that allow users to stream TV shows, movies, and other forms of entertainment directly from the internet. The best part is that many of these apps offer free content or provide access to popular streaming platforms like Netflix, Hulu, or Amazon Prime at a fraction of the cost of traditional cable TV.

To take advantage of the free and low-cost content available through smart TV apps, all you need is a stable internet connection. Simply navigate to the app store on your smart TV, browse through the available apps, and download the ones that interest you. Once installed, you can start exploring a world of entertainment options.

In addition to popular streaming platforms, smart TV apps also offer access to a plethora of free online streaming websites. These legal websites provide access to a variety of TV shows and movies without any subscription fees. From classic movies to the latest TV series, you can find a vast library of content to suit your interests.

Moreover, smart TVs can also be used to set up and utilize internet protocol television (IPTV) services. These services offer a wide range of channels at a fraction of the cost of cable TV. By following step-by-step instructions, you can easily set up and enjoy a vast selection of channels from around the world.

Furthermore, smart TVs can serve as a hub for your media library. By setting up a personal media server using a computer or a network-attached storage (NAS) device, you can stream content to multiple devices within your home. This DIY media server setup allows you to access your favorite movies, TV shows, and music on-demand, without relying on expensive cable subscriptions.

In conclusion, accessing free and low-cost content through smart TV apps is a practical and cost-effective alternative to expensive cable television. By utilizing the built-in apps and features of smart TVs, you can explore a world of entertainment options, from popular streaming platforms to free online streaming websites. Additionally, smart TVs can also be used to set up IPTV services and create a personal media server for a truly customized entertainment experience. So, why pay for expensive cable when you can access a wealth of content right at your fingertips?

Troubleshooting Common Smart TV Issues

In this subchapter, we will address some of the most common issues that users may encounter when using a smart TV. Smart TVs offer a wide range of features and functionalities, but they can also come with their fair share of technical difficulties. By understanding and troubleshooting these issues, you can ensure a smooth and hassle-free streaming experience.

One common issue with smart TVs is a slow or unstable internet connection. If you are experiencing buffering, lag, or frequent disconnections while streaming content, there are a few steps you can take to improve your connection. First, check your Wi-Fi signal strength and make sure your smart TV is within range of your router. If the signal is weak, consider moving the router closer to your TV or using a Wi-Fi extender. You can also try resetting your router or contacting your internet service provider for assistance.

Another common problem is compatibility issues with streaming apps. Some smart TVs may not support certain apps, or the apps may need to be updated to the latest version. If you are having trouble accessing a particular app, check for updates in your TV's app store or contact the app's support team for further assistance. Additionally, ensure that your TV's firmware is up to date, as outdated firmware can cause compatibility issues.

Occasionally, smart TVs may encounter software glitches or freezing. If your TV becomes unresponsive or freezes while using an app, try restarting your TV by unplugging it from the power source for a few seconds and then plugging it back in. If the issue persists, you can perform a factory reset to restore your TV to its default settings. However, keep in mind that a factory reset will erase all your personalized settings and installed apps, so make sure to back up any important data beforehand.

Lastly, if you are experiencing audio or visual issues, such as no sound or distorted picture, check your TV's audio and video settings. Ensure that the volume is not muted or too low, and adjust the picture settings according to your preferences. If the problem persists, you may need to contact the TV manufacturer's customer support for further assistance or consider seeking professional help.

By troubleshooting these common smart TV issues, you can enjoy a seamless streaming experience and make the most of your cord-cutting journey. Remember to refer to the user manual provided with your smart

TV for specific troubleshooting steps and consult online forums or communities for additional support.

Chapter 5: Discovering IPTV Services for Comprehensive Channel Selection

Introduction to IPTV: How It Works and Benefits

In today's digital age, the world of television is rapidly evolving. Gone are the days when cable TV subscriptions were the only way to access a wide range of entertainment options. With the rise of streaming services, antenna TV, and smart TVs, consumers now have a plethora of alternatives to expensive cable television. One such alternative that is gaining popularity is IPTV, or internet protocol television.

IPTV is a method of delivering television content over the internet, allowing users to stream their favorite shows and movies on-demand. It works by transmitting television signals over an internet protocol network, rather than traditional terrestrial, satellite, or cable television formats. This means that viewers can access a vast array of channels and content from around the world, all at a fraction of the cost of cable TV.

The benefits of IPTV are numerous. Firstly, it offers an extensive range of channels, including international and niche channels that may not be available through traditional cable providers. This means that viewers can enjoy a broader selection of content tailored to their specific interests.

Additionally, IPTV provides flexibility and convenience. Users can watch their favorite shows and movies at any time, on any device with an internet connection. Whether it's on a smart TV, computer, smartphone, or tablet, IPTV allows viewers to access their entertainment wherever and whenever they choose.

Furthermore, IPTV services often come with advanced features such as DVR capabilities, allowing users to record their favorite shows and watch them at their convenience. This eliminates the need to worry about missing out on live broadcasts or scheduling conflicts.

Setting up and using IPTV services is relatively straightforward. By following step-by-step instructions, users can easily install and configure the necessary software or applications on their devices. With a stable internet connection and a compatible device, viewers can start enjoying the benefits of IPTV in no time.

In conclusion, IPTV is a cost-effective and versatile alternative to expensive cable television. With its wide range of channels, flexible viewing options, and advanced features, it offers viewers a convenient and personalized entertainment experience. By exploring the world of IPTV, individuals can take control of their television viewing and enjoy a wealth of content at their fingertips.

Choosing the Right IPTV Service Provider

In today's digital age, cable television is becoming increasingly expensive, prompting many people to explore alternative options. One such alternative is internet protocol television (IPTV) services, which offer a wide range of channels at a fraction of the cost of cable TV. However, with numerous providers available, choosing the right IPTV service can be overwhelming. This subchapter aims to guide you through the process of selecting the best IPTV service provider to meet your entertainment needs.

When considering an IPTV service provider, it is essential to evaluate the channel selection they offer. Look for providers that offer a diverse range of channels, including your favorite networks and genres. Some providers also offer additional features like video-on-demand services or catch-up TV, allowing you to watch previously aired programs at your convenience.

Reliability is another crucial factor to consider. Opt for a provider that offers a stable and consistent streaming experience, ensuring minimal buffering and downtime. Reading customer reviews and testimonials can provide valuable insights into the reliability of different IPTV service providers.

The compatibility of the service with your devices is another essential aspect to consider. Ensure that the IPTV service is compatible with your smart TV, streaming device, or mobile device. Many providers also offer apps for various platforms, making it convenient to access their services.

Pricing is a significant consideration for most people looking to cut the cord. Compare the pricing plans of different IPTV service providers, considering both the monthly subscription fees and any additional costs or hidden charges. Some providers may offer discounted rates for longer-term subscriptions, so evaluate your viewing habits and budget accordingly.

Lastly, customer support and technical assistance should not be overlooked. Look for providers that offer responsive customer support, whether through live chat, email, or phone. This ensures that any issues or concerns you may have can be promptly addressed.

By taking these factors into consideration, you can make an informed decision when choosing an IPTV service provider. Remember to thoroughly research and compare different providers to find the one that best aligns with your entertainment preferences and budget. With the right IPTV service, you can enjoy a wide range of channels and content at a fraction of the cost of traditional cable television.

Setting Up and Activating Your IPTV Service

In this subchapter, we will guide you through the process of setting up and activating your IPTV service. Internet Protocol Television (IPTV) offers a wide range of channels at a fraction of the cost of cable TV, making it an attractive option for those seeking alternatives to expensive cable television. By following these step-by-step instructions, you will be able to access a plethora of channels and enjoy your favorite TV shows and movies without breaking the bank.

1. Choosing an IPTV Service Provider:

- Research different IPTV service providers and compare their offerings, pricing, and customer reviews.

- Look for providers that offer a wide variety of channels, including popular networks and international options.

- Consider factors such as streaming quality and customer support when making your decision.

2. Signing Up for an IPTV Service:

- Visit the website of your chosen IPTV service provider.

- Look for a signup or registration option and click on it.

- Fill in the required information, such as your name, email address, and payment details.

- Review the terms and conditions, and if you agree, proceed with the signup process.

3. Setting Up Your IPTV Service:

- After signing up, you will receive login credentials from your IPTV service provider.

- Download the appropriate app for your device, such as a smart TV, streaming device, or smartphone.

- Open the app and enter your login credentials to access your IPTV service.

- Follow any on-screen prompts to complete the setup process.

4. Activating Your IPTV Service:

- Once you have set up the app, you may need to activate your IPTV service.

- Visit the activation page provided by your IPTV service provider.

- Enter the activation code or login credentials provided by the provider.

- Follow any additional instructions on the activation page to complete the process.

Congratulations! You have successfully set up and activated your IPTV service. Now you can enjoy a wide range of channels and access your favorite TV shows and movies at a fraction of the cost of cable television. Remember to regularly check for updates and explore the features and settings offered by your IPTV service provider to enhance your viewing experience. Stay tuned for the next subchapter, where we will guide you through other alternatives to expensive cable television.

Navigating and Managing Channels on IPTV Platforms

In today's digital age, cable television has become increasingly expensive, leaving many people searching for alternatives to save money without sacrificing their favorite shows and movies. One such alternative is Internet Protocol Television (IPTV), which offers a wide range of channels at a fraction of the cost of cable TV. In this subchapter, we will explore how to navigate and manage channels on IPTV platforms, providing step-by-step instructions to help you make the most of this cost-effective solution.

To begin, it's important to understand what IPTV is and how it works. Unlike traditional cable or satellite TV, IPTV uses internet protocol to deliver television content, allowing you to stream channels and on-demand content directly to your television or other devices. This means you can access a vast selection of channels without the need for a cable or satellite subscription.

Setting up an IPTV service is relatively simple. First, you will need a compatible device, such as a smart TV, streaming device, or computer. Once you have your device, you can download an IPTV app or software and sign up for a service that suits your needs. There are many IPTV providers available, each offering different channel packages and features, so it's important to do your research and choose one that aligns with your preferences.

Once you have set up your IPTV service, it's time to navigate and manage the channels. IPTV platforms typically provide user-friendly interfaces that allow you to browse through the available channels and content. You can often organize channels into favorites or create custom playlists to easily access your preferred shows and movies.

Managing channels on IPTV platforms also involves understanding the various options and features available to enhance your viewing experience. For example, some IPTV services offer features like time-shifting, which allows you to pause, rewind, or fast-forward through live TV. You may also have access to an electronic program guide (EPG) that provides a schedule of upcoming shows and allows you to set reminders or record programs.

In addition to managing channels, IPTV platforms often offer additional features and services, such as on-demand content, catch-up TV, and even interactive applications. These features can further enhance your entertainment experience and provide you with more control over what you watch and when.

In conclusion, navigating and managing channels on IPTV platforms is a crucial aspect of utilizing this cost-effective alternative to cable television. By following the step-by-step instructions provided in this subchapter, you will be able to set up and optimize your IPTV service, browse through a wide range of channels, and take advantage of the various features and options available. With IPTV, you can enjoy your favorite shows and movies at a fraction of the cost of cable TV, making it a valuable option for those looking to cut the cord.

Chapter 6: Exploring Free Online Streaming Websites

Legal Websites for Free Streaming: Overview and Safety Considerations

In today's digital age, the ever-rising costs of cable television have led many individuals and families to seek alternative options for entertainment. One such alternative is free streaming, which provides access to a wide range of TV shows and movies without any subscription fees. While there are numerous websites that offer free streaming, it is important to ensure that you are accessing content legally and safely. This subchapter will provide an overview of legal websites for free streaming and highlight important safety considerations.

When it comes to free streaming, there are several reputable websites that offer a vast library of TV shows and movies. Websites like Crackle, Tubi, and Pluto TV partner with content providers to offer a range of titles that can be streamed for free. These platforms are legal and supported by advertisements, which help offset the costs of providing free content.

When utilizing legal streaming websites, it is crucial to prioritize safety. One of the key safety considerations is avoiding illegal streaming websites that offer copyrighted content without proper authorization. These websites not only violate copyright laws but also expose users to potential malware, viruses, and other security threats.

To ensure your safety while streaming, it is recommended to stick to well-known and reputable websites. These websites often have established partnerships with content providers and have measures in place to protect users from harmful content. Additionally, consider using ad-blockers or pop-up blockers to minimize the risk of encountering malicious advertisements.

Another safety consideration is the use of Virtual Private Networks (VPNs) while streaming. VPNs encrypt your internet connection and mask your IP address, providing an extra layer of security and privacy. By using a VPN, you can protect your personal information and ensure that your online activities remain private.

It is also important to be mindful of the content you stream, especially when it comes to children. Some free streaming websites may not have robust content filtering systems in place, making it essential for parents to monitor and control what their children are accessing.

In conclusion, legal websites for free streaming offer a convenient and cost-effective alternative to expensive cable television. By adhering to safety considerations and utilizing reputable platforms, you can enjoy a wide variety of TV shows and movies without compromising your security or legality.

Popular Free Streaming Websites: Features and Content Offerings

In this subchapter, we will explore the world of popular free streaming websites and delve into the features they offer and the content they provide. As alternatives to expensive cable television, these platforms have gained popularity among cord-cutters looking for cost-effective ways to enjoy their favorite TV shows and movies.

1. Variety of Content: Free streaming websites like Crackle, Tubi, and Pluto TV offer a wide variety of TV shows, movies, documentaries, and even original programming. Users can explore different genres and discover content from various decades and countries.

2. On-Demand Viewing: Unlike traditional cable television, free streaming websites allow users to watch their favorite shows and movies on-demand. This means you can watch what you want, when you want, without having to adhere to a fixed schedule.

3. No Subscription Fees: One of the major advantages of these platforms is that they are completely free. Users can access a vast library of content without the need to pay any subscription fees. This makes them an attractive option for those looking to save money while still enjoying quality entertainment.

4. Ad-Supported Model: To support their free offerings, these platforms rely on advertisements. While this may mean occasional interruptions during your viewing experience, it allows them to provide content at no cost to the user.

5. User-Friendly Interface: Most free streaming websites have intuitive and user-friendly interfaces, making it easy for even the most tech-challenged individuals to navigate and find the content they desire. These platforms often include search functionalities, personalized recommendations, and user reviews to enhance the viewing experience.

6. Legal and Safe: It is important to highlight that the free streaming websites discussed in this subchapter are legal and safe to use. They obtain the necessary licenses to distribute the content they offer, ensuring that users can enjoy their favorite shows and movies without any legal repercussions.

It is worth noting that while free streaming websites provide a wealth of content, they may not always have the latest releases or exclusive content found on subscription-based platforms like Netflix or Hulu. However, for those seeking a cost-effective alternative to cable television, these websites offer a great starting point.

In the following subchapters, we will explore other alternatives, such as antenna TV setup, smart TV apps, IPTV services, DIY media server setup, and more. By combining these various options, individuals can create a personalized and affordable entertainment ecosystem that suits their viewing preferences and budget.

Streaming TV Shows and Movies without Subscription Fees

In this subchapter, we will explore the various options available for streaming TV shows and movies without the need for expensive subscription fees. With the rise of cord-cutting and the increasing popularity of alternative options to cable television, it is now easier than ever to access your favorite content without breaking the bank.

One of the most popular alternatives to expensive cable television is the use of streaming services. Platforms like Netflix, Hulu, and Amazon Prime offer a wide range of TV shows and movies for a monthly subscription fee. However, there are also free streaming services available that provide access to a variety of content without any subscription fees. We will discuss these free streaming websites and how to access them legally.

Another option for accessing free content is through the use of antenna TV. We will provide step-by-step instructions on how to install and use an antenna to receive over-the-air channels for free. This is a great option for those who want to watch local channels and enjoy live TV without the need for a cable subscription.

Smart TVs are becoming increasingly popular, and many come with built-in apps and features that allow you to access free or low-cost content. We will provide a comprehensive guide on how to utilize these apps and features to stream your favorite TV shows and movies without the need for a subscription.

Internet Protocol Television (IPTV) services are another alternative to cable TV that offers a wide range of channels at a fraction of the cost. We will provide step-by-step instructions on setting up and using IPTV services to access a plethora of channels without the need for a cable subscription.

For those who prefer a DIY approach, we will also explore how to create a personal media server using a computer or a network-attached storage (NAS) device. This will allow you to stream content to multiple devices within your home without relying on expensive cable subscriptions.

Additionally, we will provide step-by-step instructions on how to set up and optimize popular streaming devices like Roku or Amazon Fire Stick. These devices offer access to a wide range of streaming services and can be a cost-effective alternative to cable TV.

Furthermore, we will discuss mobile streaming options, including instructions on using apps, data-saving tips, and recommended streaming services for smartphones and tablets. This will allow you to enjoy your favorite TV shows and movies on the go without the need for a cable subscription.

Lastly, we will explore the various media resources available at local libraries, such as DVDs, audiobooks, and online streaming platforms they offer for free. We will also discuss community-driven media sharing, where people can share TV shows and movies with one another for free or at a low cost through local community networks or platforms.

With these alternatives to expensive cable television, you can enjoy your favorite TV shows and movies without the burden of high subscription fees. Whether through free streaming websites, antenna TV, smart TVs, IPTV services, DIY media servers, streaming devices, mobile options, local libraries, or community-driven sharing, there are plenty of options available to suit your preferences and budget.

Tips for Finding High-Quality and Up-to-Date Content on Free Streaming Websites

As more and more people are cutting the cord and turning to free streaming websites as an alternative to expensive cable television, it is important to know how to find high-quality and up-to-date content. With so many options available, it can be overwhelming to navigate through the vast sea of websites and ensure that you are accessing legal and reliable sources. Here are some essential tips to help you find the best content on free streaming websites:

1. Research reputable websites: Start by researching and identifying reputable websites that offer free streaming services. Look for websites that have a good reputation and positive user reviews. Some well-known examples include Crackle, Tubi, IMDb TV, and Pluto TV.

2. Check for legal sources: Ensure that the websites you visit provide legal and licensed content. This will not only give you peace of mind but also protect you from any potential legal issues. Legitimate websites obtain the necessary rights to stream movies and TV shows, so always be cautious of websites that seem too good to be true.

3. Utilize user reviews and ratings: Take advantage of user reviews and ratings to gauge the quality of the content available on a specific website. This can give you valuable insights into the user experience, video quality, and reliability of the streaming service.

4. Look for recently added content: To ensure that you have access to the latest TV shows and movies, check if the website regularly updates its content library. Most reputable free streaming websites provide a section for recently added content, allowing you to stay up-to-date with the latest releases.

5. Explore genre-specific websites: If you have a specific genre or niche interest, consider exploring websites that cater to those interests. There

are numerous websites that specialize in specific genres like horror, action, or documentaries, providing a curated selection of content that aligns with your preferences.

6. Use reliable search engines: When searching for specific TV shows or movies, use reliable search engines like Google to find the most relevant and up-to-date results. Be specific in your search queries to narrow down the results and find the content you are looking for.

7. Be cautious of pop-up ads and malware: Free streaming websites often rely on ads to generate revenue. However, be cautious of excessive pop-up ads or suspicious links that could potentially lead to malware. Use ad-blockers or a reputable antivirus software to protect your device from any potential threats.

By following these tips, you can navigate through free streaming websites with confidence, ensuring that you find high-quality and up-to-date content without compromising on legality or security. Enjoy the freedom and flexibility of free streaming while saving money on expensive cable television subscriptions.

Chapter 7: Creating Your DIY Media Server

Introduction to Media Servers: Computer vs. NAS Device

In today's digital age, the options for accessing and streaming media content have expanded significantly. With the ever-rising costs of cable television, many people are seeking alternatives that offer more flexibility, affordability, and a wider range of content. One popular solution is setting up a personal media server, which allows you to stream your favorite TV shows, movies, and music to multiple devices in your home. Two common methods of creating a media server are using a computer or a network-attached storage (NAS) device. In this subchapter, we will explore the advantages and disadvantages of both options to help you make an informed decision.

Using a computer as a media server offers several benefits. Firstly, most people already own a computer, which eliminates the need for additional hardware. Additionally, computers typically have more processing power and storage capacity compared to NAS devices, allowing for smoother streaming and the ability to store a vast library of media files. However, a computer-based media server requires the computer to be powered on and running at all times, which can lead to increased energy consumption and potential noise disturbance.

On the other hand, a NAS device is specifically designed for storing and streaming media content. It offers a dedicated solution that is always on, ensuring uninterrupted access to your media. NAS devices also often come with user-friendly interfaces and built-in media server software, making setup and management relatively straightforward. However, NAS devices can be more expensive than using an existing computer, and their limited processing power may result in slower streaming speeds or difficulties handling high-resolution media files.

Ultimately, the choice between using a computer or a NAS device as your media server depends on your individual needs and preferences. If you already have a capable computer and don't mind keeping it powered on, using it as a media server can be a cost-effective option. On the other hand, if you prefer a dedicated solution that is always available and don't mind the additional expense, a NAS device might be the better choice.

Regardless of which option you choose, setting up a media server can significantly enhance your cord-cutting experience. It allows you to access a vast library of content, customize your media streaming setup, and enjoy the freedom of choosing what, when, and where to watch. By understanding the differences between using a computer and a NAS device as your media server, you can make an informed decision that best suits your needs and budget. So, let's dive in and explore the world of DIY media server setup!

Choosing the Right Hardware for Your DIY Media Server

In today's digital age, the popularity of cable television is declining as more and more people are cutting the cord in search of alternatives that are both cost-effective and offer a wider range of content. One such alternative is setting up a DIY media server, which allows you to stream your favorite TV shows, movies, and other media content to multiple devices within your home network. However, to create a seamless streaming experience, it is crucial to choose the right hardware for your DIY media server setup.

The first consideration when selecting hardware for your media server is the storage capacity. Depending on your needs and budget, you can either use an old computer with a large hard drive or invest in a network-attached storage (NAS) device. A NAS device not only provides ample storage space but also offers additional features such as remote access and data redundancy.

Another important factor to consider is the processing power of your media server. This is especially crucial if you plan on transcoding or converting media files on the fly. Look for a device with a powerful processor and sufficient RAM to ensure smooth streaming without any buffering or lag.

Connectivity options are also essential. Ensure that your media server has sufficient USB ports, Ethernet ports, and Wi-Fi capabilities to connect to your devices and network seamlessly. Additionally, having an HDMI output can come in handy if you want to connect your media server directly to your TV or home theater system.

When it comes to software compatibility, consider choosing a hardware device that supports popular media server software such as Plex, Emby, or Kodi. These software solutions offer user-friendly interfaces, media organization tools, and support for a wide range of file formats.

Lastly, keep in mind the scalability and future-proofing of your media server setup. Look for hardware that allows for easy expansion of storage or the addition of more devices in the future. Additionally, consider devices that receive regular firmware updates to ensure compatibility with the latest streaming technologies and security patches.

By carefully considering these factors, you can choose the right hardware for your DIY media server setup, ensuring a smooth and enjoyable streaming experience for you and your family. Whether you opt for a computer-based setup or a dedicated NAS device, selecting the right hardware is crucial to unlock the full potential of your media server and enjoy a wide range of content without the hassle and expense of traditional cable television.

Setting Up and Configuring Your Media Server

In this subchapter, we will explore the process of setting up and configuring your own media server, which will allow you to stream content to multiple devices within your home network. By creating a personal media server, you can have full control over your media library and access it anytime, without relying on expensive cable TV subscriptions.

To get started, you will need either a computer or a network-attached storage (NAS) device. If you choose to use a computer, ensure that it has enough storage space to accommodate your media files. If you opt for a NAS device, make sure it is compatible with media server software. Popular options include Plex, Emby, and Kodi.

Once you have chosen your hardware, follow these steps to set up your media server:

1. Install the media server software: Download and install the media server software of your choice on your computer or NAS device. These software options are typically free and offer user-friendly interfaces.

2. Organize your media library: Before adding your media files to the server, organize them in a way that makes sense to you. Create separate folders for TV shows, movies, music, etc. This will help you easily locate and access your content.

3. Add media files to the server: Use the media server software to add your media files to the server. You can do this by selecting the folders where your files are stored and letting the software scan and categorize them automatically.

4. Configure server settings: Customize your media server settings according to your preferences. This may include setting up user accounts,

enabling remote access, and optimizing streaming quality based on your network's capabilities.

5. Connect devices to the server: Install the media server app on the devices you want to stream content to. This can be your smart TV, smartphone, tablet, or even a gaming console. Ensure that all devices are connected to the same Wi-Fi network as your media server.

6. Enjoy your media library: Once everything is set up, you can now access and stream your media library on any connected device. Browse your collection, create playlists, and enjoy your favorite TV shows, movies, and music without the need for cable TV subscriptions.

Creating your own media server allows you to have complete control over your entertainment options. You can add new content, customize your viewing experience, and save money by cutting the cord on expensive cable TV subscriptions. Take the time to set up and configure your media server, and you'll soon be enjoying a vast library of content on your terms.

Streaming Content to Multiple Devices: Tips and Troubleshooting

As more and more people seek alternatives to expensive cable television, streaming content has become a popular choice. Not only does it offer a wide range of options for TV shows and movies, but it also allows viewers to access their favorite content on multiple devices. However, streaming to multiple devices can sometimes be a bit tricky. In this subchapter, we will provide you with tips and troubleshooting techniques to ensure a seamless streaming experience.

1. Bandwidth Considerations: One of the most important factors to consider when streaming to multiple devices is your internet bandwidth. Make sure your internet plan can handle streaming on multiple devices

simultaneously. Check with your internet service provider for any necessary upgrades to avoid buffering or slow streaming.

2. Router Placement: The placement of your router plays a crucial role in ensuring a strong and consistent Wi-Fi signal throughout your home. Position it centrally to maximize coverage and reduce dead spots. Avoid placing it near walls, metal objects, or other electronic devices that may interfere with the signal.

3. Wi-Fi Signal Strength: A weak Wi-Fi signal can lead to buffering and poor streaming quality. Boost your Wi-Fi signal by using a range extender or mesh Wi-Fi system. These devices can help eliminate dead zones and provide a stronger signal to all your devices.

4. Device Limitations: Different devices have varying capabilities when it comes to streaming content. Older devices may struggle to handle high-quality streams or multiple streams simultaneously. Consider upgrading your devices if you frequently experience lag or poor video quality.

5. Network Prioritization: Prioritize your streaming devices on your network to ensure a smooth streaming experience. Many routers offer Quality of Service (QoS) settings that allow you to allocate more bandwidth to specific devices, such as smart TVs or streaming devices.

6. Troubleshooting Common Issues: If you encounter issues with streaming on multiple devices, perform basic troubleshooting steps such as restarting your router, clearing cache and cookies on your devices, or updating your streaming apps. These simple steps can often resolve common issues.

By following these tips and troubleshooting techniques, you can enjoy a seamless streaming experience on multiple devices. Whether you're using popular streaming platforms like Netflix, Hulu, or Amazon Prime, or exploring alternatives like antenna TV setup, IPTV services, or DIY media servers, streaming content to multiple devices can be a convenient and cost-effective alternative to expensive cable television. Stay connected, entertained, and informed with the plethora of streaming options available to you.

Remember, technology is constantly evolving, so staying informed and updated on the latest streaming trends and devices will help you make the most of your streaming experience. Happy streaming!

Chapter 8: Optimizing Roku or Fire Stick for Streaming

Introduction to Roku and Amazon Fire Stick: Features and Capabilities

In today's digital age, cable television has become increasingly expensive, pushing many individuals and families to seek alternatives. With the rise of streaming services and advancements in technology, there are now more options than ever to enjoy your favorite TV shows and movies without breaking the bank. In this subchapter, we will explore two popular streaming devices – Roku and Amazon Fire Stick – and delve into their features and capabilities.

Roku and Amazon Fire Stick are compact streaming devices that connect to your television and provide access to a wide variety of streaming services, including popular platforms like Netflix, Hulu, and Amazon Prime. These devices offer a convenient and cost-effective way to stream content directly to your TV, eliminating the need for expensive cable subscriptions.

One of the key features of Roku and Amazon Fire Stick is their user-friendly interface. With a simple setup process, you can quickly connect the device to your TV and navigate through different apps and services with ease. Both devices offer a wide range of channels and streaming options, allowing you to customize your viewing experience based on your preferences.

Furthermore, Roku and Amazon Fire Stick come with voice search capabilities, making it even easier to find the content you're looking for. Simply speak into the remote control and let the device do the searching for you. This feature is especially handy when you have a specific movie or TV show in mind but don't want to spend time scrolling through endless options.

Another advantage of these streaming devices is their compatibility with other smart home devices. By connecting your Roku or Amazon Fire Stick to your smart home ecosystem, you can control your TV and streaming experience with voice commands or through smartphone apps. This integration adds an extra layer of convenience to your cord-cutting journey.

In conclusion, Roku and Amazon Fire Stick are powerful streaming devices that offer a plethora of features and capabilities to enhance your cord-cutting experience. Whether you're a tech-savvy individual or a novice in the streaming world, these devices are designed to provide a seamless transition from traditional cable television to a more affordable and flexible way of accessing your favorite content. Stay tuned as we dive deeper into the setup and optimization process of these two devices, ensuring you get the most out of your streaming experience.

Setting Up Your Roku or Fire Stick Device

In today's digital age, there are countless alternatives to expensive cable television that can save you money without sacrificing your favorite shows and movies. One popular option is to use streaming devices like Roku or Amazon Fire Stick. These devices allow you to access a plethora of streaming services, giving you the freedom to choose what you want to watch and when you want to watch it. In this subchapter, we will guide you through the process of setting up and optimizing your Roku or Fire Stick device.

To begin, you will need to connect your streaming device to your TV. Both Roku and Fire Stick come with an HDMI cable that you can use to do this. Simply plug one end of the cable into the HDMI port on your

TV and the other end into the corresponding port on your device. Once connected, make sure your TV is set to the correct input channel.

Next, you will need to connect your device to the internet. Roku and Fire Stick can both be connected to your Wi-Fi network. Simply follow the on-screen instructions to connect to your network and enter your Wi-Fi password if prompted. It's important to have a stable internet connection for seamless streaming.

After connecting to the internet, you will need to create or sign in to your Roku or Amazon account. This will allow you to access and manage your streaming services. If you don't have an account, you can easily create one for free.

Once you're logged in, you can start adding your favorite streaming services to your device. Roku and Fire Stick offer a wide range of channels and apps that you can browse and install. From popular streaming platforms like Netflix, Hulu, and Amazon Prime to free online streaming websites, there's something for everyone.

To optimize your streaming experience, you can explore additional features and settings on your device. For example, you can customize your home screen, adjust display settings, and enable closed captions. These settings can enhance your viewing experience and make it more tailored to your preferences.

In conclusion, setting up your Roku or Fire Stick device is a simple and straightforward process that can open up a world of entertainment options. By following these step-by-step instructions, you'll be well on your way to enjoying the benefits of cord-cutting and saving money on expensive cable television. So go ahead, grab your remote and start exploring the endless possibilities of streaming services.

Customizing and Managing Streaming Apps on Roku or

Fire Stick

Streaming devices have revolutionized the way we consume entertainment, providing a cost-effective alternative to expensive cable television. Among the most popular streaming devices are Roku and Amazon Fire Stick, both offering an array of streaming apps and features. In this subchapter, we will delve into customizing and managing streaming apps on these devices to enhance your cord-cutting experience.

Setting up your Roku or Fire Stick is a breeze, requiring only a stable internet connection and an HDMI port on your TV. Once connected, you can access a plethora of streaming services like Netflix, Hulu, or Amazon Prime. However, the true power of these devices lies in their customization options.

Both Roku and Fire Stick allow you to personalize the content you see by rearranging app icons and creating customized menus. This means you can prioritize your favorite streaming apps and hide ones you rarely use, providing a seamless, personalized streaming experience.

Furthermore, these devices offer voice control features, allowing you to search for content using simple voice commands. Whether you're looking for a specific movie or genre, just speak into the remote and let the device do the rest. This not only saves time but also makes navigating through the vast collection of streaming apps effortless.

Managing your streaming apps also includes keeping them up to date. Roku and Fire Stick regularly release software updates that enhance performance, security, and add new features. It's essential to check for updates regularly and install them to ensure the best streaming experience.

Additionally, you can explore the extensive app stores of Roku and Fire Stick to discover new streaming services. These platforms offer a wide selection of free or low-cost apps that cater to various niches and interests. From sports and news to niche content and international channels, the possibilities are endless.

In conclusion, customizing and managing streaming apps on Roku or Fire Stick is crucial to optimize your cord-cutting experience. By personalizing your app layout, utilizing voice control, and staying up to date with software updates, you can create a seamless, tailored streaming experience. Explore the vast app stores, discover new services, and take advantage of the numerous features these devices offer. With Roku or Fire Stick, the world of streaming entertainment is at your fingertips.

Troubleshooting Common Issues with Roku or Fire Stick

Introduction:

Roku and Amazon Fire Stick are popular streaming devices that offer a wide range of entertainment options as alternatives to expensive cable television. However, like any technology, they can sometimes encounter issues that hinder the viewing experience. In this subchapter, we will address common problems that users may face with Roku or Fire Stick and provide step-by-step troubleshooting instructions to help you resolve them quickly and easily.

1. Device Setup and Connectivity Issues:

- Difficulty in setting up the device or connecting it to the TV or Wi-Fi network.

- Step-by-step instructions on how to perform a factory reset and reconnect the device.

2. Streaming Quality and Buffering Problems:

- Frequent buffering or poor video quality while streaming content.

- Tips to optimize your internet connection and adjust streaming settings for smoother playback.

3. App Installation and Performance Issues:

- Problems with installing or updating apps on your streaming device.

- Troubleshooting steps to resolve app crashes, freezes, or slow performance.

4. Remote Control Problems:

- Issues with the remote control not working or not responding.

- Troubleshooting tips for re-pairing the remote or replacing the batteries.

5. Audio and Video Compatibility:

- Troubles with audio or video not syncing properly or displaying in the wrong format.

- Instructions on adjusting audio and video settings for optimal playback.

6. Firmware Updates and System Errors:

- Error messages or system glitches that may occur during firmware updates.

- Steps to troubleshoot and resolve firmware update failures or system errors.

Conclusion:

By following the troubleshooting instructions provided in this subchapter, you can resolve common issues that may arise with Roku or Fire Stick and ensure a seamless streaming experience. Remember, with a bit of patience and the right guidance, you can overcome any obstacles and enjoy the benefits of cord-cutting without the expensive cable television.

Chapter 9: Streaming TV on the Go: Mobile Options

Exploring Mobile Streaming Apps: Netflix, Hulu, and More

In today's digital age, cable television has become increasingly expensive, prompting many people to seek alternative options for entertainment. Streaming services have gained immense popularity as a viable alternative to cable TV, offering a wide range of TV shows, movies, and other content at a fraction of the cost. This subchapter delves into the world of mobile streaming apps, with a focus on popular platforms such as Netflix, Hulu, and more.

Mobile streaming apps have revolutionized the way we consume media, allowing us to enjoy our favorite shows and movies on the go. Netflix, the industry giant, offers an extensive library of content, including original series and blockbuster movies. Hulu, on the other hand, provides a combination of current TV shows, classic series, and original content. Other noteworthy mobile streaming apps include Amazon Prime Video, Disney+, and HBO Max, each offering their own unique selection of content.

In this subchapter, we will provide step-by-step instructions on how to access and utilize these mobile streaming apps. We will guide you through the process of downloading and installing the apps on your smartphone or tablet, ensuring that you have the best possible streaming experience. Additionally, we will offer data-saving tips to help you optimize your streaming habits and avoid exceeding your mobile data limits.

Furthermore, we will explore the various subscription options available for these mobile streaming apps, including free trials and discounted plans. We will also discuss the compatibility of these apps with different operating systems and devices, ensuring that you can stream your favorite content no matter what device you own.

Whether you're a cord-cutter looking for alternatives to expensive cable television or simply seeking the convenience of streaming on your mobile device, this subchapter will provide you with all the information you need. By exploring the world of mobile streaming apps such as Netflix, Hulu, and more, you can unlock a vast array of entertainment options at your fingertips. So sit back, relax, and let us guide you through the exciting world of mobile streaming.

Managing Data Usage and Saving Costs on Mobile Streaming

In today's digital age, mobile streaming has become increasingly popular as people seek convenient and affordable alternatives to expensive cable television. With the rise of smartphones and tablets, streaming TV shows and movies on-the-go has never been easier. However, it's important to manage data usage and save costs to ensure a seamless and budget-friendly streaming experience.

Firstly, it is essential to choose the right streaming service that offers data-saving options. Many popular streaming platforms like Netflix, Hulu, and Amazon Prime provide settings that allow you to adjust video quality to consume less data. By choosing a lower resolution or enabling data-saving modes, you can significantly reduce your data usage without compromising on the viewing experience.

Furthermore, it's advisable to connect to a reliable Wi-Fi network whenever possible. Streaming over Wi-Fi does not consume your mobile data, making it an excellent way to save costs. Take advantage of free Wi-Fi hotspots in coffee shops, libraries, or even your workplace to enjoy your favorite shows and movies without worrying about data usage.

To optimize data usage, consider downloading content for offline viewing. Most streaming services offer the option to download TV episodes or movies, allowing you to watch them later without an internet connection. This not only saves data but also ensures uninterrupted entertainment during commutes or while traveling.

Another cost-saving tip is to keep track of your data usage by using your mobile provider's data monitoring tools or third-party apps. These tools can help you identify data-hungry apps or streaming services and make necessary adjustments to minimize data consumption.

Lastly, consider subscribing to a mobile plan that offers unlimited streaming or data rollover options. Many mobile providers now offer plans specifically tailored for streaming enthusiasts, allowing them to enjoy unlimited streaming without worrying about exceeding data limits or incurring additional charges.

By implementing these strategies, you can effectively manage your data usage and save costs on mobile streaming. Whether you're using a smartphone or tablet, streaming TV shows and movies on the go has never been more accessible and affordable. Embrace the freedom of cord-cutting and enjoy your favorite content without breaking the bank.

Optimizing Video Quality and Performance on Mobile Devices

In today's digital age, mobile devices have become an integral part of our lives. People now rely on their smartphones and tablets for various activities, including streaming TV shows and movies. However, when it comes to enjoying high-quality video content on these devices, there can be some challenges. This subchapter aims to provide valuable insights and tips on how to optimize video quality and performance on mobile devices, ensuring a seamless streaming experience.

First and foremost, it is crucial to have a reliable and fast internet connection. Slow or unstable connections can result in buffering issues and poor video quality. Therefore, it is recommended to connect to a Wi-Fi network whenever possible, as it typically offers faster speeds and more stability compared to cellular data.

Another important factor to consider is the video resolution. Higher resolutions, such as 1080p or even 4K, require more bandwidth and may not be suitable for mobile devices with smaller screens. Adjusting the video resolution to match the screen size can significantly improve performance and reduce data consumption. Most streaming platforms offer options to change the video quality settings, so it's worth exploring these settings and finding the right balance between quality and performance.

In addition to resolution, it is essential to consider the streaming app or platform being used. Some apps may have additional settings specifically designed for mobile devices, such as data-saving modes or adaptive streaming. These features can help optimize video playback and reduce data usage, especially when streaming on the go.

Furthermore, clearing the cache and closing unnecessary apps in the background can also enhance video streaming performance. Mobile devices have limited resources, and freeing up memory and processing power can improve overall performance, resulting in smoother playback and faster loading times.

Lastly, it is worth mentioning the importance of keeping mobile devices up to date. Regular software updates often include bug fixes and performance improvements that can positively impact video streaming. Additionally, updating the streaming apps themselves ensures access to the latest features and optimizations.

By following these tips and tricks, users can optimize video quality and performance on their mobile devices, enabling them to enjoy their favorite TV shows and movies seamlessly. Whether streaming at home or on the go, these optimizations will ensure a fantastic viewing experience without the need for expensive cable television.

Recommended Mobile Streaming Services and Content Selection

As more and more people are cutting the cord and seeking alternatives to expensive cable television, mobile streaming has become a popular option for accessing a wide range of TV shows and movies on the go. In this subchapter, we will explore the recommended mobile streaming services and provide guidelines for selecting the best content to suit your preferences.

When it comes to mobile streaming, there are several popular platforms to choose from. Netflix, Hulu, and Amazon Prime are the most well-known and widely used services, offering a vast library of TV shows and movies that can be accessed anytime, anywhere. These platforms provide a seamless streaming experience on smartphones and tablets, allowing you to catch up on your favorite shows or discover new content while on the move.

For those looking for free alternatives, there are also options available. Free online streaming websites offer legal access to a variety of TV shows and movies without any subscription fees. However, it's essential to be cautious and choose reputable websites to ensure a safe and legal streaming experience.

When selecting content for mobile streaming, it's important to consider your preferences and interests. Whether you enjoy binge-watching TV shows, exploring documentaries, or keeping up with the latest movies, these platforms offer a wide variety of genres and categories to cater to every taste. Additionally, some services provide personalized recommendations based on your viewing history, making it easier to discover new content that aligns with your interests.

To optimize your mobile streaming experience, it's recommended to utilize data-saving tips. Streaming video content can consume a significant amount of data, so it's advisable to connect to a Wi-Fi network whenever possible to avoid exceeding your data plan. Furthermore, adjusting the streaming quality to a lower resolution can help reduce data usage without compromising the viewing experience.

In conclusion, mobile streaming has revolutionized the way we consume TV shows and movies, providing flexibility and convenience to viewers. By selecting the right streaming service and content, you can enjoy a wide range of entertainment options right at your fingertips. Whether you prefer popular streaming platforms, free online streaming websites, or community-driven media sharing, there are plenty of options available to cater to your preferences. So grab your smartphone or tablet and start exploring the world of mobile streaming today!

Chapter 10: Leveraging Local Library Resources

Discovering Media Resources at Your Local Library

In an age where cable television is becoming increasingly expensive, many people are turning to alternative options to satisfy their entertainment needs. While streaming services and smart TV apps are popular choices, one often overlooked resource is the local library. Libraries offer a plethora of media resources that can be accessed for free or at a low cost, making them an excellent option for those looking to cut the cord on expensive cable television.

One of the main advantages of utilizing your local library is the wide range of media options available. Most libraries have an extensive DVD collection, including popular TV shows and movies, allowing you to enjoy your favorite content without the need for a cable subscription. Additionally, many libraries offer audiobooks, which are perfect for those who prefer to listen to their favorite stories on the go.

Furthermore, libraries have embraced the digital age and now offer online streaming platforms as well. Through partnerships with services like Kanopy or Hoopla, library patrons can access a vast catalog of movies, documentaries, and TV shows from the comfort of their own homes. These platforms are completely free to use with a library card, providing an affordable alternative to expensive cable subscriptions.

To take full advantage of the media resources at your local library, it's important to familiarize yourself with the library's catalog and policies. Most libraries have an online catalog where you can search for specific titles or browse different categories. Additionally, libraries often have rental periods for DVDs or online streaming platforms, so it's essential to know how long you can keep the media before returning it.

Visiting your local library can also be a great way to discover new content that you may not have been aware of otherwise. Libraries often have curated collections or staff recommendations, allowing you to explore different genres and expand your horizons. Whether you're interested in classics, foreign films, or the latest TV series, your local library is sure to have something to suit your tastes.

In conclusion, discovering media resources at your local library is an excellent option for those looking to cut the cord on expensive cable television. With a wide range of DVDs, audiobooks, and online streaming platforms available for free or at a low cost, libraries provide a cost-effective and accessible alternative. By taking advantage of the media resources offered by your local library, you can enjoy your favorite TV shows, movies, and more without breaking the bank.

Accessing DVDs and Blu-rays for Free

In this subchapter, we will explore the various ways you can access DVDs and Blu-rays for free, allowing you to enjoy your favorite movies and TV shows without the need for an expensive cable television subscription. Whether you prefer physical copies or simply want to expand your viewing options beyond streaming services, this guide will provide you with step-by-step instructions on how to access DVDs and Blu-rays at no cost.

One of the easiest and most accessible options is utilizing your local library resources. Many libraries offer an extensive collection of DVDs and Blu-rays that you can borrow for free. Simply visit your local library, sign up for a library card, and browse their collection. Most libraries have a wide range of genres and titles to choose from, ensuring there is something for everyone.

Another option is to explore community-driven media sharing platforms. These platforms allow individuals to share their personal

DVD and Blu-ray collections with others in the community. By joining or creating a local network, you can connect with like-minded individuals who are willing to share their media content with you. This not only gives you access to a greater variety of movies and TV shows but also fosters a sense of community and connection.

If you prefer the convenience of streaming but still want to access DVDs and Blu-rays, consider setting up a DIY media server. With a computer or a network-attached storage (NAS) device, you can create your own personal media server. This allows you to digitize your DVD and Blu-ray collection and stream them to multiple devices within your home network. This option requires some technical know-how, but the benefits are worth it if you have a large physical media collection.

Lastly, don't forget about the power of online platforms. While many streaming services require a subscription, there are legal websites that offer free access to a variety of TV shows and movies. These websites often include older titles or independent films that may not be available on popular streaming platforms. By exploring these options, you can find hidden gems and expand your viewing horizons without breaking the bank.

In conclusion, accessing DVDs and Blu-rays for free is not only possible but also offers a range of benefits. Whether you utilize your local library, join a community-driven sharing platform, set up a DIY media server, or explore free online streaming websites, you can enjoy a vast selection of movies and TV shows without the need for an expensive cable television subscription. By taking advantage of these alternatives, you can cut the cord and embrace a more affordable and flexible approach to entertainment.

Exploring Audiobooks and Digital Media Offerings

In today's digital age, the world of entertainment has expanded beyond traditional cable television. With the rise of audiobooks and various digital media offerings, there are now countless alternatives to expensive cable television. This subchapter will delve into the exciting realm of audiobooks and digital media, providing you with the knowledge and tools to access a wide range of content at a fraction of the cost.

Audiobooks have become increasingly popular, allowing individuals to enjoy their favorite books while on the go. Whether you are driving, exercising, or simply relaxing at home, audiobooks offer a convenient way to immerse yourself in captivating stories. With platforms like Audible, you can access a vast library of audiobooks and enjoy them at your own pace. This subchapter will guide you through the process of setting up an audiobook account, choosing the right audiobooks for your interests, and maximizing your listening experience.

Additionally, we will explore the world of digital media offerings, including streaming services, smart TV apps, and IPTV services. Streaming services like Netflix, Hulu, and Amazon Prime have revolutionized the way we consume television shows and movies. We will provide step-by-step instructions on how to set up and navigate these popular platforms, ensuring you make the most of your streaming experience.

For those looking for a more traditional television experience, we will guide you through the process of setting up an antenna TV. This cost-effective option allows you to access free over-the-air channels, providing a range of local and national programming. We will provide detailed instructions on how to install and use an antenna, ensuring you never miss your favorite shows.

In addition to these options, we will explore DIY media server setups, Roku or Fire Stick setups, mobile streaming options, and community-driven media sharing. These innovative approaches offer even more possibilities for accessing free or low-cost content.

Lastly, we will discuss the resources available at local libraries, such as DVDs, audiobooks, and online streaming platforms. Many libraries now offer free access to a variety of media, providing an excellent alternative to expensive cable television.

By exploring audiobooks and digital media offerings, you will gain a comprehensive understanding of the numerous alternatives to expensive cable television. This subchapter will empower you to take control of your entertainment choices, saving you money while still enjoying a wide range of captivating content. Whether you prefer audiobooks, streaming services, or community-driven media sharing, there is an option for everyone. Let's embark on this exciting journey together and discover the world of audiobooks and digital media.

Utilizing Online Streaming Platforms Provided by Libraries

In today's digital age, where cable television costs are skyrocketing, it is becoming increasingly important to explore alternative options for entertainment. One such option that many people overlook is the vast array of online streaming platforms provided by libraries. These platforms offer a treasure trove of free movies, TV shows, documentaries, and more, all at your fingertips.

To access these online streaming platforms, all you need is a library card. Most libraries have partnered with popular streaming services like Kanopy, Hoopla, and OverDrive to offer their patrons a wide range of digital content. By utilizing these platforms, you can enjoy a wealth of entertainment without having to spend a dime.

Kanopy is a popular streaming platform that offers a diverse collection of movies, documentaries, and educational content. With a library card, you can stream thousands of titles, including classic films, independent cinema, and award-winning documentaries. Whether you're a film buff or just looking for something new to watch, Kanopy has something for everyone.

Hoopla, on the other hand, focuses on providing a vast selection of eBooks, audiobooks, comics, music, and movies. With no wait times and simultaneous access, you can instantly stream or download your favorite content to enjoy offline. From best-selling novels to the latest Hollywood blockbusters, Hoopla has it all.

OverDrive is another fantastic platform that offers a wide range of eBooks, audiobooks, and videos. With OverDrive, you can borrow digital content from your local library and access it on your preferred device, whether it's a smartphone, tablet, or eReader. The best part is that the borrowed content automatically returns itself, so you never have to worry about late fees.

By taking advantage of these online streaming platforms provided by libraries, you can cut the cord on expensive cable television subscriptions and still have access to a wealth of entertainment options. Whether you're a fan of movies, TV shows, documentaries, or books, these platforms have something for everyone.

So, grab your library card and start exploring the world of online streaming. With just a few clicks, you can immerse yourself in a world of free and low-cost entertainment that will keep you entertained for hours on end. Say goodbye to expensive cable television and hello to the vast resources of your local library.

Chapter 11: Building Community-Driven Media Sharing Platforms

Joining Existing Community Networks for Media Sharing

In today's digital age, cable television has become increasingly expensive, leading many people to seek out alternative options for their entertainment needs. One such option is joining existing community networks for media sharing. These networks provide a platform for individuals to connect with like-minded individuals and share their favorite shows, movies, and media content without the hefty price tag associated with cable television.

Joining an existing community network for media sharing is a simple and cost-effective way to access a wide range of content. These networks are usually formed by individuals who are passionate about a particular genre or type of media, such as classic movies, documentaries, or TV series. By joining these networks, you gain access to a vast library of content that is shared among the members.

To get started, you'll need to search for existing community networks that align with your interests. There are various online platforms and forums where you can find these networks. Look for communities that are active and have a good track record of sharing high-quality content. Once you find a community that piques your interest, you can request to join or follow their guidelines to become a member.

Once you become a member of a community network, you can start exploring and sharing content. Most networks have a system in place for members to contribute and access media. This may involve uploading your own content or simply accessing content shared by others. You can browse through the available media, download what interests you, and even contribute your own collection to enrich the network further.

Joining an existing community network for media sharing not only provides you with access to a vast library of content but also opens up opportunities for social interaction. You can connect with like-minded individuals who share your passion for specific shows, movies, or genres. Many networks have forums or chat rooms where you can discuss and exchange recommendations with other members, creating a sense of community and camaraderie.

In conclusion, joining existing community networks for media sharing is an excellent alternative to expensive cable television. It offers a cost-effective way to access a wide range of content while connecting with like-minded individuals. By taking advantage of these networks, you can enjoy your favorite shows and movies without breaking the bank. So, why wait? Start exploring and joining community networks today and take control of your entertainment options.

Creating Local Platforms for Sharing TV Shows and Movies

In today's digital age, there are countless alternatives to expensive cable television, allowing consumers to access their favorite TV shows and movies without breaking the bank. One innovative option that has gained popularity is the creation of local platforms for sharing media content. These platforms provide a unique opportunity for the public to come together and exchange their favorite TV shows and movies, either for free or at a low cost.

One such option is community-driven media sharing, where individuals join or create local networks or platforms dedicated to sharing media content. These platforms can be physical, such as local DVD lending libraries, or virtual, utilizing online platforms or social media groups. By participating in these community-driven initiatives, individuals can access a wide array of TV shows and movies without the need for expensive cable subscriptions.

Another avenue for sharing TV shows and movies locally is through local libraries. Many libraries now offer not only physical DVDs but also access to online streaming platforms, providing a wealth of content for library patrons at no additional cost. By utilizing these resources, individuals can enjoy their favorite TV shows and movies without the need for expensive cable providers or subscription services.

Furthermore, individuals can create their own local platforms for sharing TV shows and movies. This can be achieved through the establishment of local media sharing networks, where like-minded individuals come together to exchange media content. These networks can be facilitated through online forums, social media groups, or even physical meetups. By pooling their resources and sharing their collections, participants can access a wide range of content without the need for costly subscriptions.

In conclusion, the creation of local platforms for sharing TV shows and movies offers a practical and affordable alternative to expensive cable television. By participating in community-driven media sharing, utilizing local library resources, or establishing their own local networks, individuals can access a plethora of content without breaking the bank. Whether it's through DVDs, online streaming platforms, or personal collections, these local platforms provide a cost-effective way for the public to enjoy their favorite TV shows and movies.

Establishing Guidelines and Rules for Community Media Sharing

In today's digital age, there are numerous alternatives to expensive cable television that provide access to a wide range of content at a fraction of the cost. One such alternative is community-driven media sharing, where individuals come together to share their favorite TV shows and movies with one another for free or at a low cost. However, it is important to establish guidelines and rules to ensure a smooth and fair sharing experience for everyone involved.

1. Respect Copyright Laws: It is crucial to emphasize the importance of respecting copyright laws when engaging in community media sharing. Encourage members to only share content that they have the legal right to distribute, such as public domain movies or content they have created themselves.

2. Obtain Permission: If members wish to share copyrighted content, they should seek permission from the original creators or obtain the necessary licenses to do so. This will prevent any legal issues and ensure that content creators are appropriately compensated for their work.

3. Set Clear Sharing Guidelines: Establish guidelines for how content should be shared within the community. This may include rules on file formats, quality standards, and the maximum number of downloads or streams allowed per user. Clear guidelines will help prevent misunderstandings and ensure a fair distribution of content.

4. Encourage Active Participation: Encourage members to actively participate in the community by sharing their own content and engaging in discussions. This will foster a sense of community and create a sustainable sharing ecosystem.

5. Create a Rating and Review System: Implement a rating and review system to allow members to provide feedback on shared content. This will help others make informed decisions about what to watch and promote high-quality content within the community.

6. Protect Personal Information: Emphasize the importance of privacy and encourage members to respect each other's personal information. Advise against sharing personal details or engaging in any form of harassment or cyberbullying.

7. Monitor and Moderate: Assign moderators or administrators to monitor the community and ensure that guidelines are followed. They should address any issues or conflicts that arise promptly and fairly.

By establishing clear guidelines and rules for community media sharing, individuals can come together to enjoy a variety of TV shows and movies at a minimal cost. This subchapter provides step-by-step instructions on how to join or create local community networks or platforms for media sharing, as well as tips for fostering a respectful and sustainable sharing environment. With the right guidelines in place, community-driven media sharing can be a valuable alternative to expensive cable television.

Engaging and Collaborating with Other Community Members for Shared Content

In today's digital age, cutting the cord and finding alternative options to expensive cable television has become increasingly popular. As a cord-cutter, you can not only save money but also gain access to a wide range of content through various streaming services, IPTV, and online platforms. However, one aspect that often goes unnoticed is the power of engaging and collaborating with other community members for shared content. By joining or creating local community networks or platforms, you can tap into a wealth of shared media content, such as TV shows or movies, for free or at a low cost.

One way to engage with other community members is through community-driven media sharing platforms. These platforms allow individuals to connect with like-minded people in their local area who are interested in sharing and exchanging media content. By joining such platforms, you can not only access a vast library of TV shows and movies but also contribute your own collection for others to enjoy. This collaborative approach not only expands your content options but also fosters a sense of community and connection among fellow cord-cutters.

Another avenue for collaboration is utilizing local library resources. Most libraries offer a plethora of media resources, including DVDs, audiobooks, and online streaming platforms, all available for free. By exploring these resources, you can access a wide range of content, from classic movies to popular TV shows, without any subscription fees. Additionally, libraries often host community events, workshops, or film screenings, providing an opportunity to connect with other cord-cutters in your area.

Furthermore, engaging with other community members through online forums, social media groups, or local meetups can be a valuable source of shared content recommendations. By actively participating in these communities, you can exchange ideas, seek advice, and discover hidden gems that may not be easily accessible through mainstream streaming services. Sharing your own recommendations and experiences can also contribute to the collective knowledge and help others in their cord-cutting journey.

In conclusion, engaging and collaborating with other community members for shared content is an excellent way to enhance your cord-cutting experience. By joining community-driven media sharing platforms, utilizing local library resources, and actively participating in online forums or meetups, you can expand your content options, build connections, and contribute to a vibrant cord-cutting community. Embrace the power of collaboration and discover a world of shared content at your fingertips.